Guidelines for the Treatment of Victims of Crime

Best Practice

Commonwealth Secretariat

Commonwealth Secretariat
Human Rights Unit
Marlborough House
Pall Mall
London
SW1Y 5HX

Telephone: +44(0)20 7747 6423
Facsimile: +44(0)20 7747 6418
Web site: http//www.thecommonwealth.org

ISBN: 0-85092-725-0

Published by the Commonwealth Secretariat
Designed by Something Big Ltd
Printed in the United Kingdom by Commercial Press PLC
Wherever possible, the Commonwealth Secretariat uses paper sourced from sustainable forests or from sources that minimise a destructive impact on the environment.

Copies of this publication can be ordered from:
The Publications Manager,
Communications and Public Affairs Division,
Commonwealth Secretariat,
Marlborough House,
Pall Mall, London SW1Y 5HX
United Kingdom
Tel: +44(0)20 7747 6342
Fax: +44(0)20 7839 9081
Email: r.jones-parry@commonwealth.int

Price: £8.99
ISBN: 0 85092-725-0

Website: www.thecommonwealth.org

Contents

Background

In November 1985, the United Nations General Assembly adopted the *Declaration of Basic Principles of Justice for Victims of Crime and Abuse of Power* (the Basic Principles) (see Annex A). This had been agreed at the UN Congress on the Prevention of Crime and the Treatment of Offenders held earlier that year in Milan, Italy. The General Assembly noted that:

> "... millions of people throughout the world suffer harm as a result of crime ... and that the rights of these victims have not been adequately recognized".

It added that:

> "... victims of crime ... and also frequently their families, and others who aid them, are unjustly subjected to loss, damage or injury and that they may, in addition, suffer hardship when assisting in the prosecution of offenders".

The Basic Principles, therefore, represented a major advance in that, for the first time, the rights of victims of crime were expressly recognised in an international document. Whilst the UN Declaration does not have binding lega effect, it represents a commitment by member states to the Basic Principles.

Since then, Canada, South Africa, the United Kingdom and some Australian states have initiated some significant administrative and legislative measures designed to protect victims' rights and interests. Some other Commonwealth countries also make limited provision for assisting victims of crime. For example, the Criminal Procedure Codes of several countries provide victims with a right to payment of compensation and restitution of property upon conviction of the offender. Of course this does not apply where the offender is not identified or is not convicted and in any event does not prescribe mandatory service standards expected of those working in the criminal justice agencies.

The overall effect is that 18 years after the UN Declaration, victims of crime in the majority of the 54 Commonwealth member states still receive little effective statutory or administrative protection or assistance.
The Commonwealth is now addressing the issue of victims of crime. Senior Officials of [Commonwealth] Law Ministries at their 2001 meeting in London welcomed this development and noted that:

> "... victims of crime can be subjected to unjust loss, damage or injury and that, in addition, they may suffer hardship when assisting in the prosecution of offenders".

They concluded that it was appropriate that Commonwealth Law Ministers be asked to consider the issue of how best to afford justice to victims of crime and recommended for their consideration a draft Commonwealth statement (see Annex B).

The development of *Commonwealth Guidelines on Best Practice for the Treatment of Victims of Crime* (hereinafter referred to as 'the Guidelines') is another significant step, not least because there is a need to build on the Basic Principles which themselves lack detail and use very general language. The advantage of developing specifically *Commonwealth* Guidelines lies in the fact that the criminal justice system(s) of almost every Commonwealth Member State uses an adversarial system with its rules of criminal procedure and criminal evidence being based on Common Law. Even countries with a Roman-Dutch law tradition make extensive use of common law principles on criminal procedure and criminal evidence.

The Expert Group

In July 2002 an expert group was convened by the Commonwealth Secretariat Human Rights Unit and met at Marlborough House in London. It was tasked with drawing up 'Best Practice Guidelines for the Treatment of Victims of Crime.' It comprised members from developed and developing countries and large and small jurisdictions from around the Commonwealth.

The following people gave freely of their time, expertise and extensive experience in developing these Guidelines.

Chief Emmanuel Akomaye Agim, Director of Public Prosecutions, The Gambia

Selina Goulbourne, School of International Studies and Law, Coventry University, Coventry, UK

John Hatchard, General Secretary, Commonwealth Legal Education Association

Robin Palmer, School of Law, University of Natal, Durban, South Africa

Gene Pestaina, Legal Practitioner and former Director of Public Prosecutions, Roseau, Dominica

Orlando G Rubene, General Secretary, Office of the Attorney General, Maputo, Mozambique

Robert J Sibley, Faculty of Law, Queensland University of Technology, Brisbane, Australia

Joe Silva, Principal, Sri Lanka Law College, Colombo, Sri Lanka

Miriam Titterton, Northern Ireland Human Rights Commission, Belfast, UK

They were assisted by officers of the Human Rights Unit, Commonwealth Secretariat.

About The Guidelines

The Guidelines provide a model legal and administrative framework through which Commonwealth member states can address the needs of victims of crime.

In developing the Guidelines, the Expert Group was conscious of the historical neglect of the rights of victims of crime. This stemmed in large part from a pre-occupation with the presumption of innocence and the development of an adversarial system whereby the public represented by the State (or its equivalent) is "pitted" against the accused represented by the defence and has largely failed to include any consideration of victims' needs and interests at every stage of the criminal justice process.

The Guidelines describe what assistance and treatment, as a minimum, victims of crime should expect from the criminal justice system, including the mandatory service standards expected of the criminal justice agencies and related government agencies.

The Expert Group was conscious of the human and economic constraints of many Commonwealth member countries and has sought to reflect this in the Guidelines. Particular care was taken to ensure that the Guidelines have few financial implications for states and to highlight areas in which victim support groups and/or civil society organisations might provide significant assistance.

The Expert Group adopted a thematic approach in developing the Guidelines to allow for a more structured analysis. In doing so, it was recognised that some responsibilities may overlap, depending upon the role and powers of different agencies within the criminal justice system of the individual state.

The Guidelines are divided into seven parts:

- Part 1: Fundamental Principles
- Part 2: Duties of Law Enforcement Officials
- Part 3: Duties of Prosecutors
- Part 4: Duties of the Court
- Part 5: Rights of Victims at the Post-Sentencing Stage
- Part 6: Compensation and Restitution
- Part 7: General Policy Issues.

The Expert Group recognised that whilst the Guidelines have no binding legal effect, they represent a commitment by Commonwealth countries to the principles stated therein and set out a model legal and administrative framework that emphasises the structural similarity on the treatment of victims of crime in member states.

The Guidelines do not specifically address the position of vulnerable victims (such as children) and victims of sexual crimes at the trial stage. In view of the work of the Commonwealth Expert Working Group on Evidence, it was felt unnecessary to do more than support its recommendations for dealing with such victims. These recommendations are set out below in Annex C.

Fundamental Principles

1.1 In these Guidelines, "victims of crime" (also called "Victims") are defined as "Persons who have suffered harm, including physical or mental injury or trauma or economic loss through acts or omissions that are in violation of the national criminal law. These include dependants and members of the immediate family of the direct victim". A person may be considered a victim regardless of whether the perpetrator is identified, apprehended, prosecuted or convicted.
[This definition approximates to the UN Declaration of Basic Principles of Justice for Victims of Crime and Abuse of Power. The Guidelines adopt a broad definition of the term "Victims of crime" to include, where appropriate, dependants and members of the immediate family of the direct victim. The Guidelines are also confined to victims of criminal acts and do not extend to victims of the political abuse of power.
The Guidelines also cover individuals who have suffered loss or injury as a result of criminal acts or omissions of person(s) who cannot be found or have not been convicted.]

1.2 Commonwealth countries recognise the historical neglect of the rights and interests of victims of crime.

1.3 Commonwealth countries should include in their national constitution or legislation appropriate measures for the protection of victims of crime.

1.4 All agencies within the criminal justice system must observe the rights of victims of crime.

1.5 The rights of victims of crime should not conflict with the rights of the accused.
[Care must be taken not to dilute or undermine the constitutional and other legal rights of suspects, detained, arrested or accused persons through establishing the protection of victims' rights.]

1.6 The rights of victims of crime should include:
- to be treated with courtesy, respect, fairness and dignity;
- to offer information and to be heard;
- to receive information;

- to privacy and protection;
- to assistance;
- to an effective and efficient investigation of the crime;
- to timely processing of criminal proceedings following the arrest of the accused.

1.7 Commonwealth countries should develop a "Charter of Victim's Rights" that should be made widely available.
["Availability" implies availability to the public at large, to victims of crime and to all those working in the criminal justice system and those in victim support structures, including the NGO community.]

1.8 Relevant government policies should support the rights of victims of crime. Where appropriate, governments should conduct impact assessment exercises in relation to policies that affect or may affect victims of crime.

1.9 Parliamentarians should consider the impact of any proposed legislation on victims of crime.

1.10 There is a need to develop effective victim support programmes.
[It is envisaged that victim support programmes will be developed by government agencies, victim support groups and civil society groups.]

1.11 States should implement these Best Practice Guidelines, amongst other things, by providing adequate training and sensitising of all officials of criminal justice agencies to the needs of victims of crime.

1.12 There is a need to avoid procedural abuses and shortcomings in the criminal justice system that can amount to secondary victimisation.

1.13 The duties of law enforcement officials, prosecutors and judicial officers that follow in these Guidelines are intended to help prevent the secondary victimisation of victims of crime.

Duties of Law Enforcement Officials

2.1 "Law enforcement officials" include members of national, regional or local police services or any other department, office or agency of the State or a statutory body with powers to investigate violations of the criminal law.
[In many Commonwealth jurisdictions, policing powers are not exclusively exercised by members of the police force. The definition here is broad enough to cover all officials engaged in crime detection and investigation.]

2.2 Law enforcement officials shall have a duty to support victims of crime to the fullest extent possible in accordance with the applicable law and practices in that jurisdiction and in light of these Guidelines.
[The rights set out below imply a corresponding duty of victims to keep the relevant authorities informed of all changes of address and (where applicable) a contact telephone number/email address.]

In particular:

1. Law enforcement officials must treat all victims of crime with courtesy, respect, fairness and dignity and in a way that is responsive to age, gender, race, ethnic, cultural, religious, political and linguistic differences or disability or other special need.

2. At the earliest opportunity, a victim of crime shall be entitled to receive the following information from law enforcement officials:
   - the name, rank and contact details of the officer to whom the complaint about the crime is made;
   - the case number/reference number;
   - the name, rank and contact details of the investigating officer;
   - upon request, a copy of the statement made to the reporting officer, or written reasons for a refusal to register the complaint.

   [The experience in some Commonwealth jurisdictions is that law enforcement officials sometimes refuse to take or act on a complaint leaving the victim powerless to advance the matter short of bringing a private prosecution (which is notoriously difficult to mount) or resorting to "instant justice". A victim's rights must be spelled out here to ensure accountability.]

3. (a) Where practicable, law enforcement officials must inform the victims of crime of the date, place and time of any bail proceedings.

[In terms of the general definition of "victim" there may be a large number of victims of any crime, thus placing an unacceptable administrative burden on law enforcement officials. The qualification "where practicable" allows the relevant official to exercise his/her discretion in deciding which victims to inform. These will usually be the direct victim(s) of the crime. Alternatively, there should be a system whereby a "representative victim" of the group victimised could be identified to accept information and act on behalf of the group.]

(b) Where practicable, law enforcement officials must inform victims of crime of the outcome of bail applications.

[This information will usually be given to the victims who have a direct interest in knowing whether or not a suspect is in custody, for example to enable them to take precautions against attacks, intimidation, etc.]

4. Law enforcement officials must provide victims of crime with information about the procedure for investigating the crime and, upon request, inform victims periodically on the status of the criminal investigation.

[The information could be provided in the form of a leaflet, brochure or pamphlet produced by a victim support organisation or other civil society body. By "status" is meant the stage of the criminal investigation that has been reached, the progress of current investigations and the likely duration until the matter reaches the trial stage.]

5. Law enforcement officials must, as soon as reasonably possible, inform victims of crime of relevant support agencies and programmes.

[The details of relevant support agencies and programmes should be made readily available to law enforcement officials in the form of a leaflet, brochure, or pamphlet that can be given to victims. These might be provided by a victim support organisation or other civil society body.]

6. Law enforcement officials must, as a general rule,

(a) establish procedures, in association with the prosecuting authorities, to ensure the release of the property belonging to victims of crime as soon as possible;

(b) inform victims of crime of the reasons for non-release of that property;

(c) inform victims of crime when a decision is taken not to release the property of the procedure for safekeeping, early release or return of their property.

[For example, victims should be informed of any statutory procedures for recovering property where its release is refused e.g. applications to a magistrate.]

7. Law enforcement officials must allow victims of crime to add to or amend their initial statement or to make a further statement.
[This duty is intended to cater for differing practices throughout the Commonwealth. In some jurisdictions victims are not permitted to write their statements themselves and are reliant on the version taken down by the law enforcement official. In some cases law enforcement officials may even refuse to include matters that are regarded as important to the victim. In such cases, victims should have the right to insist on clarifications or additions or to state their version in their own words.]

8. Law enforcement officials must inform victims of crime of their right to apply for compensation under any applicable compensation schemes (if any) or to seek restitution.
[Information about any pre-trial and post-trial victim compensation schemes and restitution should be readily available in the form a leaflet, brochure, or pamphlet that can be given to victims. These might be provided by a victim support organisation or other civil society body.]

9. In cases of sexual offences or other crimes involving life-threatening diseases, particularly HIV/AIDS or hepatitis B, law enforcement officials must immediately assist victims of crime to obtain medical testing and preventative medical measures and inform them of any appropriate counselling facilities.
[This recognises that there is a need for pro-active efforts in cases where the time frame for preventative measures may be as short as 24 hours (e.g. where a victim may have been infected with the HIV/AIDS virus). In such cases law enforcement officers must receive adequate training to deal with such situations.]

10. Law enforcement officials must protect the privacy of victims of crime, and scrupulously ensure that the laws and practices protecting the victim as a complainant or witness are observed.
[This duty goes beyond merely observing existing laws and practices: the privacy of victims who are not protected by such laws or practices must also be vigorously protected. See also the commentary to 4.1 below.]

11. Law enforcement officials must take all reasonable measures to protect victims from violence, intimidation or harassment. This includes informing the victim should an alleged offender escape from lawful custody, abscond whilst on bail or otherwise be released from official custody.

12. As soon as reasonably possible after the detection of a crime the law enforcement official in charge of the investigation must:
    (a) with reference to the definition of 'victim' contained Part 1, identify all victims of the crime;
    (b) compile a list of the identified victims of the crime;
    (c) amend the list from time to time as new victims are identified.

    [The duties of law enforcement officials are spelled out in detail due to the importance of avoiding disputes about who may and may not lay claim to "victim" status. It is intended that this list of victims should become an official document on the police docket and should be given an official police standing orders reference number or equivalent. Failure to adhere to these requirements will otherwise adversely affect the operation of these Guidelines and any Charter of Victims' Rights, as law enforcement officials will be able to avoid their duties to protect victims by merely alleging that they did not consider a particular person to be a "victim".
    The duty under paragraph 12(c) is intended to cater for situations where new persons who qualify for the status of "victim" are identified in the course of the criminal investigation, trial or post-trial proceedings.]

13. Law enforcement officials should provide victims with an information pack detailing the general rights of victims.
    [This information pack should also contain the information envisaged under paragraphs 5 and 8 above. Again these might be produced by a victim support organisation or other civil society group.]

Duties of Prosecutors

3.1 "Prosecutors" shall include any person entrusted with the duty to prosecute a criminal matter.
[This takes into account the fact that in some Commonwealth jurisdictions the handling of committal hearings and even the prosecution of offences before summary courts is handled by members of a law enforcement agency.]

3.2 Every victim has the right, at any stage of the criminal justice process, to make representations in writing to the relevant prosecuting authority about any matter, and to receive a written reply giving reasons for the decisions taken.
[This shall include the right to make representations to the superior of a prosecutor with whom the victim is dissatisfied.]

3.3 Prosecutors have a duty to support victims of crime to the fullest extent possible in accordance with applicable laws and practices and in light of these Guidelines.

This support shall be based on the following principles:

1. Prosecutors must treat all victims of crime with courtesy, respect, fairness and dignity and in a way that is responsive to age, gender, race, ethnic, cultural, religious, political and linguistic differences or disability or other special need.

2. Prosecutors must take into consideration the views of the victim(s) when considering whether a prosecution is in the public interest;

3. Victims must have the right:
   (a) to be informed, prior to the commencement of the trial, of the final charges to be preferred against the accused and the reasons for any amendment to the original charge(s);
   [The victim is entitled to know if (and the reasons why) the final charge(s) differ from the original charge(s) investigated against the accused. For example, where a "rape" complaint is reduced to a final charge of "assault".]

(b) to be informed as soon as possible of any decision not to proceed with or to discontinue the prosecution of the case;

(c) to be informed as soon as possible of any decision to proceed with the matter through non-trial procedures;

[Non-trial procedures differ from jurisdiction to jurisdiction and may include pre-trial diversion programmes, plea bargains and sentencing agreements, referral for mental observation and any institutionalised alternative dispute resolution mechanisms.]

(d) to be informed, should they not be satisfied with any of the decisions taken in (a) (b) or (c) above, of the right to make representations to the superior of the prosecutor concerned.

[These rights imply a corresponding duty of victims to keep the relevant authorities informed of all changes of address and (where applicable) a contact telephone number/email address.]

4. Upon request, prosecutors must inform victims of the status of the criminal matter.

5. Prosecutors must, at all stages of the criminal process, ensure that the privacy of the victim is protected and scrupulously ensure that the laws and practices protecting the victim as a complainant or witness are observed.
   [See commentary in part 4.1 below.]

6. Where practicable:
   (a) prosecutors must inform victims of crime of the date, place and time of any bail proceedings;
   [In terms of the general definition of "victim" there may be a large number of victims of any crime, thus placing an unacceptable administrative burden on prosecutors. The qualification "where practicable" allows flexibility, taking into account logistical constraints, but does not take away the general duty to inform the victim(s). These will usually be the direct victim(s) of the crime. Alternatively, there may be a system whereby a "representative victim" of the group victimised could be identified to accept information and act on behalf of the group.]

(b) prosecutors must inform victims of crime of the outcome of bail applications;
[This information will usually be given to the victims who have a direct interest in knowing whether or not a suspect is in custody, for example to enable them to take precautions against attacks or intimidation.]

7. Prosecutors should ensure, as far as possible, that victims proceeding to court, at court and whilst leaving court, are protected against unwanted contact occurring between such persons and the accused or anyone associated with the alleged offender.
[This is to prevent so-called "silent intimidation" such as sustained eye contact and intentional jostling passed off as accidental contact.

8. Prosecutors must as far as is practicable take steps to ensure that victims are familiarised with court procedures and conduct in court.
[It is important that victims are informed of the stages of the trial and what is required of them. This should extend to the layout of the court and the role of the court officers. A victim to be called as a witness should receive detailed instructions, whereas more general information would suffice for non-witness victims. Such a task could be delegated to court officials or a victim support organisation.]

9. In addressing the court on sentence, the prosecutor has a duty to place before the court all relevant information about the victim. In addition the prosecutor must inform the court of all monetary compensation options available in terms of the law and practice, and, if required, the prosecutor must assist the victim to claim compensation.
[Compensation may be available to victims at two stages of the process. Firstly, compensation may become available at the sentencing stage when it becomes part of the sentence imposed. Secondly, it may be available under a statutory victim relief/compensation fund. (see Part 6 below).]

10. In serious cases a prosecutor must inform the victim that she/he has a right to make or provide information for the making of a Victim Impact Statement. This statement may include information on the financial, social, psychological, and medical impact of the crime upon the victim and the victim's family.

[This gives practical expression to the victim's right to offer information and to be heard. The practices in Commonwealth jurisdictions vary from those where there is no provision made for the receipt of a Victim Impact Statement to those where the process is highly formalised, for example, where the victim completes a detailed questionnaire and has the right to present the statement personally to the court.]

11. Prosecutors must inform victims of the noting of any appeal and the outcome of that appeal.

Duties of the Court

["The court" means both the presiding judicial officer or any assessors who may constitute part of the bench.]

4.1 Judicial officers must scrupulously ensure that the laws and practices protecting the victim as a complainant or witness are observed.
[The court should be vigilant to take pro-active steps to protect the victim as a complainant/witness. In the case of certain vulnerable witnesses (e.g. children, victims of sexual attack, persons from minority groups) the general principle that justice should be dispensed in open court should give way to the need to prevent secondary victimisation. Where they have not already done so, Commonwealth countries should consider enshrining into legislation the recommendations on "Vulnerable Witnesses" included in the Commonwealth Secretariat Report of the Expert Working Group on Evidence (2001). These are contained in Annex C.]

4.2 Judicial officers must treat all victims of crime with courtesy, respect, fairness and dignity and in a way that is responsive to age, gender, race, ethnic, cultural, religious, political and linguistic differences or disability or other special need.
[Appropriate provisions could be included in Judicial Codes of Conduct that are now becoming increasingly popular throughout the Commonwealth. All training programmes should ensure that court officers and officials are sensitive to the needs of victims.]

4.3 In deciding a suitable sentence, a judicial officer should take into account the impact of the crime upon the victim. With the consent of the victim a judicial officer may require a Victim Impact Statement to be obtained where the Prosecutor has failed to provide one.

4.4 When an offender is convicted, the judicial officer should always consider the question of compensation for the victim and restitution.
[Paragraphs 4.3-4.4 should form part of the standard sentencing principles and should be enshrined in legislation.]

4.5 The judicial officer must, in deciding whether to postpone or adjourn or otherwise dispose of a criminal matter, give full consideration to the interests of the victim.

Rights of Victims at the Post–Sentencing Stage

5.1 Victims must have the right to be informed of a parole or similar hearing, and to receive details of the premature release of the prisoner(s) detained or imprisoned for a serious offence against them.
[This right implies a corresponding duty of victims to keep the relevant authorities informed of any change of address and (where applicable) a contact telephone number/email address. A "serious offence" is left for definition by individual Commonwealth jurisdictions.]

5.2 Victims must have the right to be heard in private at parole or similar hearings.
[The right to be "heard" means not only the right to consult with a legal representative and to be represented or accompanied at the hearing by a lawyer or representative of a victim support group, but also the right to make a personal statement, orally or in writing to the Parole Board at the hearing itself. The duty to protect the rights in both paragraph 5.1 and 5.2 should lie with the corrective (prison) authorities.]

Compensation and Restitution

[The following provisions apply to victim compensation/restitution schemes.]

6.1 Member states should set up and develop a statutory victim relief/compensation fund. The relief or compensation is intended to help the victim and is not intended to reflect the compensation to which the victim may be entitled under law.
[The type of relief or compensation fund and the amount of assistance that can be offered will depend upon the resources available (and the availability of other financial assistance e.g. through a social security scheme). Thus such funds may differ greatly between Commonwealth countries. The amount of help that may be available to a victim (or their family) in terms of such funds may therefore vary from nominal compensation (e.g. paying medical or funeral expenses only) to more extensive relief, including perhaps compensation for emotional damage. It must also be borne in mind that a relief fund may not necessarily be confined to providing monetary compensation. Other forms of relief, such as free counselling, free rehabilitation programmes, may also be considered.]

6.2 Compensation should be expressly distinguished from damages in a civil action.
[In this regard therefore, compensation under the fund does not affect the victim's right to damages under civil law and the victims must be informed of this.]

6.3 States should put in place options for compensation for victims of crime in their legislation.

6.4 States should consider restitution as an additional sentencing option. Where appropriate, offenders should make fair restitution to victims and their families.

6.5 State sponsored victim relief schemes should generally be limited to victims of violent crime.
[This does not preclude the use of such schemes for non-violent property offences where this is thought appropriate and is financially possible.]

6.6 States should make provision for the victims' rights to compensation either on their application or on the court's own motion.

6.7 Independent human rights commissions or victim support groups should assist victims to seek redress.

6.8 The right to claim compensation should be extended to the dependants of deceased victims of crime.

6.9 Legislation should provide the right for the court to award compensation to direct victims of a crime of violence who have suffered material loss or personal injury as a result of the crime.
[Direct victims shall include the dependents of persons killed as a result of the crime and for the reimbursement of persons responsible for funeral expenses. These awards may be made upon application by the prosecutor or the victim or by the court on its own motion.]

General Policy Issues

[This Part deals with other relevant issues of a policy nature.]

7.1 States should establish an independent overseeing mechanism or office for victims within the criminal justice system with the responsibility of protecting and promoting the interests of victims.

7.2 States should introduce effective sanctions for a failure of those working in the criminal justice system to comply with their duties with respect to victims' rights.
[Commonwealth states should establish an office dedicated to ensuring effective compliance with the duties towards victims set out in these Guidelines. This office (e.g. "Victims' Ombudsman" or "Victims' Rights Officer") need not spawn an expensive new bureaucracy. It may be a part of an existing agency (e.g. a Human Rights Commission, Office of the Ombudsman or Police Complaints Ombudsman) or may be delegated to a victim support group or a civil society body specifically established for this purpose.]

7.3 States should encourage the setting up of victim support groups.
[These already operate in several Commonwealth countries and offer comfort, support (both short and long-term) and practical advice to victims. As noted in these Guidelines, they may also help to provide general information to victims. The groups can also play a useful overseeing role in the protection of the rights of victims within the criminal justice system. Consideration might also be given to encouraging the setting up of self-help support groups for the surviving relatives of homicide victims.]

7.4 Governments should ensure adequate co-ordination between criminal justice agencies, social welfare bodies and relevant victim support organisations and structures.
[Networking and sharing of information among these bodies should be supported and encouraged.]

7.5 Suitable training on victims' rights should be provided for all those working within the criminal justice system.

7.6 States should provide a conducive court environment for victims and their families who attend the trial.
[For example, ensuring that, as far as practicable, court officials establish separate waiting rooms for prosecution and defence witnesses]

7.7 States should establish appropriate mechanisms to protect children from possible re-offending by released prisoners convicted of offences against children.
[This might include placing the offender on a Sex Offenders Register or the like.]

7.8 States should establish and develop, where appropriate, restorative justice programmes and Alternative Dispute Resolution (ADR) mechanisms which will help the victims of crime.

7.9 States should commission research on the rights of victims and encourage a sharing of information between Commonwealth states.

7.10 The Commonwealth should support the development of research projects on victims of crime.

Annex A

UN Declaration of Basic Principles of Justice for Victims of Crime and Abuse of Power

A. Victims of Crime

1. "Victims" means persons who, individually or collectively, have suffered harm, including physical or mental injury, emotional suffering, economic loss or substantial impairment of their fundamental rights, through acts or omissions that are in violation of criminal laws operative within member states, including those laws proscribing criminal abuse of power.

2. A person may be considered a victim, under this Declaration, regardless of whether the perpetrator is identified, apprehended, prosecuted or convicted and regardless of the familial relationship between the perpetrator and the victim. The term "victim" also includes, where appropriate, the immediate family or dependants of the direct victim and persons who have suffered harm in intervening to assist victims in distress or to prevent victimisation.

3. The provisions contained herein shall be applicable to all, without distinction of any kind, such as race, colour, sex, age, language, religion, nationality, political or other opinion, cultural beliefs or practices, property, birth or family status, ethnic or social origin, and disability.

Access to justice and fair treatment

4. Victims should be treated with compassion and respect for their dignity. They are entitled to access to the mechanisms of justice and to prompt redress, as provided for by national legislation, for the harm that they have suffered.

5. Judicial and administrative mechanisms should be established and strengthened where necessary to enable victims to obtain redress through formal or informal procedures that are expeditious, fair, inexpensive and accessible. Victims should be informed of their rights in seeking redress through such mechanisms.

6. The responsiveness of judicial and administrative processes to the needs of victims should be facilitated by:
Informing victims of their role and the scope, timing and progress of the proceedings and of the disposition of their cases, especially where serious crimes are involved and where they have requested such information;
Allowing the views and concerns of victims to be presented and considered at appropriate stages of the proceedings where their personal interests are affected, without prejudice to the accused and consistent with the relevant national criminal justice system;
Providing proper assistance to victims throughout the legal process;
Taking measures to minimise inconvenience to victims, protect their privacy, when necessary, and ensure their safety, as well as that of their families and witnesses on their behalf, from intimidation and retaliation;
Avoiding unnecessary delay in the disposition of cases and the execution of orders or decrees granting awards to victims.

7. Informal mechanisms for the resolution of disputes, including mediation, arbitration and customary justice or indigenous practices, should be utilised where appropriate to facilitate conciliation and redress for victims.

Restitution

8. Offenders or third parties responsible for their behaviour should, where appropriate, make fair restitution to victims, their families or dependants. Such restitution should include the return of property or payment for the harm or loss suffered, reimbursement of expenses incurred as a result of the victimisation, the provision of services and the restoration of rights.

9. Governments should review their practices, regulations and laws to consider restitution as an available sentencing option in criminal cases, in addition to other criminal sanctions.

10. In cases of substantial harm to the environment, restitution, if ordered, should include, as far as possible, restoration of the environment, reconstruction of the infrastructure, replacement of community facilities and reimbursement of the expenses of relocation, whenever such harm results in the dislocation of a community.

11. Where public officials or other agents acting in an official or quasi-official capacity have violated national criminal laws, the victims should receive restitution from the state whose officials or agents were responsible for the harm inflicted. In cases where the Government under whose authority the victimising act or omission occurred is no longer in existence, the state or Government successor in title should provide restitution to the victims.

Compensation

12. When compensation is not fully available from the offender or other sources, states should endeavour to provide financial compensation to:
    (a) Victims who have sustained significant bodily injury or impairment of physical or mental health as a result of serious crimes;
    (b) The family, in particular dependants of persons who have died or become physically or mentally incapacitated as a result of such victimisation.

13. The establishment, strengthening and expansion of national funds for compensation to victims should be encouraged. Where appropriate, other funds may also be established for this purpose, including those cases where the state of which the victim is a national is not in a position to compensate the victim for the harm.

Assistance

14. Victims should receive the necessary material, medical, psychological and social assistance through governmental, voluntary, community-based and indigenous means.

15. Victims should be informed of the availability of health and social services and other relevant assistance and be readily afforded access to them.

16. Police, justice, health, social service and other personnel concerned should receive training to sensitise them to the needs of victims, and guidelines to ensure proper and prompt aid.

17. In providing services and assistance to victims, attention should be given to those who have special needs because of the nature of the harm inflicted or because of factors such as those mentioned in paragraph 3 above.

Annex B

Treatment of Victims of Crime. Draft Commonwealth Statement for Consideration by Law Ministers

Commonwealth Law Ministers recall the adoption by the United Nations General Assembly of Resolution 40/34 which recognised "that the victims of crime and the victims of abuse of power, and also frequently their families, and others who aid them, are unjustly subjected to loss, damage or injury and that they may, in addition, suffer hardship when assisting in the prosecution of offenders" and the adoption of the Declaration of Basic Principles of Justice for Victims of Crime and Abuse of Power (the Basic Principles).

To express their commitment to the Basic Principles, Ministers agree that member countries would give consideration to the national implementation of measures designed to give practical effect to these Principles. They believe that:

1. Guidelines and training programmes should be developed to ensure that **Police**:
   - are sensitive to the needs of victims;
   - are informed, knowledgeable, and supportive of existing social services and programmes for victims;
   - establish procedures in association with prosecuting authorities for the prompt return of property to victims. Alternative methods of procuring evidence such as the taking of photographs to be used as evidence should be determined; and
   - establish procedures to ensure that victims of crime are periodically informed of the status of investigations.

2. **Prosecutors,** in the exercise of their powers and duties as officers of the court:
   - should be sensitised to the fact that public interest should specifically take into consideration the views of victims;
   - have the ultimate responsibility for informing victims of the status of a case from the time of the initial court appearance to the conclusion of the case;

- have an obligation to bring to the attention of the court the views of victims of violent crime on bail decisions, postponements, plea bargains, dismissal of cases and restitution;
- should charge and pursue defendants who harass, threaten, injure or otherwise attempt to intimidate or retaliate against victims or witnesses;
- should use a victim and witness on-call system, where practicable, to ensure that victims do not waste time unnecessarily in court;
- establish procedures to ensure the prompt return of victim's property, and in so far as is possible, do away with the need for the actual physical evidence to be produced in court;
- establish and maintain liaison with victim support structures; and
- be sensitised to the trauma and well-being of victims of serious crimes.

3. **Parole Boards,** in the performance of their functions, should give consideration to:
   - notifying victims of crime and their families in advance of parole hearings as far as is practicable;
   - allowing victims of crime, their families, or their representatives to attend parole hearings and make known the effect of the offender's crime on them; and
   - taking whatever steps are necessary to ensure that parolees charged with a crime whilst on parole are immediately returned to custody and kept there until the case is adjudicated.

4. Law Ministers also commend for the consideration of the Chief Justice and other members of the **Judiciary** the following suggestions that they believe will assist in the achievement of national adherence to the Basic Principles:
   - participation in a training programme addressing the needs and legal interest of victims of crime;
   - allowing victims and witnesses to be on-call for court proceedings;
   - in so far as possible, ensuring that their court officials establish separate waiting rooms for prosecution and defence witnesses;
   - means by which members of the judiciary can bear their share of responsibility for reducing court congestion by ensuring that all participants fully and responsibly utilise court time;
   - allowing a victim to make representations at bail hearings, postponements, plea bargains, withdrawal of cases by prosecutors, and restitution;

- ordering restitution to the victims in all cases in which the victim has suffered material loss or physical or mental harm, unless they state compelling reasons for a contrary ruling on the record;
- allowing the victim and a member of the victim's family to attend the trial, even if identified as witnesses, unless there is a compelling need to the contrary; and
- giving substantial weight to the victim's interest in the speedy return of property before trial in ruling on the admissibility of photographs of that property as being sufficient evidence.

5. Ministers also agree that they should give consideration to the passage, where necessary or appropriate, of legislation that will assist in the realisation of adherence to the Basic Principles. To this end they recognise that national legislation and practice should be reviewed to:
   - ensure that it does not inhibit the ability of courts and justice authorities to allow the views of victims of violent crime to be considered on bail decisions, postponements, plea bargains, withdrawal of cases by the prosecutor and restitution;
   - facilitate the receipt by courts of Victim Impact Statements prior to sentencing;
   - require consideration of restitution in all cases; and
   - provide guidance on the fair treatment of victims of crime and witnesses.

They further agreed that national consideration should be given to the development of appropriate mechanisms designed to provide assistance to the victims. They recognise that the precise form such mechanisms could take must remain a matter for national decision, taking into account the economic, social and cultural norms of each member country.

Annex C

Extracts from Report of the Expert Working Group on Evidence (Commonwealth Secretariat, 2001)

IV VULNERABLE WITNESSES *[footnotes omitted]*

The group discussed the issue of special legislative provisions addressing vunerable witnesses and recommended the following provisions for a model law.

i. Definition of Vulnerable Witness

A vulnerable witness means a witness, whose ability to give evidence or the quality of whose evidence is likely to be affected by one or more of the following factors.

(a) age or maturity;

(b) physical, intellectual, or psychiatric disability;

(c) trauma suffered by the witness;

(d) the witness's fear of intimidation;

(e) the linguistic or cultural background of the witness;

(l) the nature of the proceeding;

(g) the nature of the evidence that the witness is expected to give;

(h) the relationship of the witness to any party to the proceeding;

(i) the absence of the witness from (name of country);

(j) any other ground of similar nature.

The Group was of the view that the term "vulnerable witness" should be broadly defined, using a non-exhaustive list of factors that a court could consider in determining if any particular witness should be considered as "vulnerable" in a specific case. The Group recommended in that regard the factors listed in the New Zealand Law Reform Commission document. The Group considered that such an approach would provide flexibility and ensure that all types of witnesses can be protected as may be necessary.

ii Application for directions by the Court

Because of the special vulnerability of children, particularly those who are the victims of violent offences, the Group was of the view that they should always be considered to be vulnerable and their evidence should be given using a measure that will avoid a face-to-face confrontation with the accused. The Group recommended a mandatory provision to that effect for children who are complainants in the case.

The Group was of the view that such measures should also be available to other witnesses that may fall within the definition of "vulnerable witness" in a particular case. The Group recommended a section empowering the judge to direct the use of special measures in relation to particular witnesses.

The Group considered whether the use of such measures should also be mandatory in the case of victims of serious sexual offences. Ultimately the Group decided that the matter was not as clear as with children. There may be circumstances where such measures would not be appropriate for an adult complainant even in a serious sexual offence case. At the same time, the Group did consider that some form of presumption should apply in the case of such witnesses, so that such measures would automatically be considered in every case of this nature. The Group recommended that in the case of such witnesses, the prosecution should be obligated to make an application to the court for special measures to apply. However, the Group also recognised that an adult complainant should be able to waive the requirement and choose to face the accused without the use of any special measure.

iii. Measures available in the case of vulnerable witnesses

(a) *The judge may direct under Section 2 that:*

(i) the witness gives evidence while in the courtroom but unable to see the defendant or specified party or witness by virtue of a screen or other device provided that the screen or other device does not prevent the witness from seeing or being seen by

1) the judge and/or jury;

2) the legal representatives acting in the proceedings; and

3) any interpreter or other person appointed to assist.

(ii) the witness gives evidence from an appropriate place outside the courtroom, either in (name of jurisdiction) or elsewhere by means of technology which allows for the witness to see and hear a person in the courtroom and be seen and heard by the persons listed above;

(iii) a video recording of an interview of the witness, or a portion thereof made before the hearing be admitted as evidence in chief;

(iv) where the examination in chief is tendered in accordance with subparagraph (iii), cross-examination and any re-examination be video recorded and any such recording or a portion thereof be admitted as the witness' evidence on cross-examination or re-examination;

(v) no person other then those specified above and the accused, be present in the courtroom during the giving of the testimony;

(vi) the wearing of wigs or gowns be dispensed with during the giving of the evidence;

(vii) the examination, cross-examination and/or re-examination of the witness be conducted through an interpreter or other person approved by the court;

(viii) the witness be assisted in the giving of evidence by a person approved by the court; or

(ix) the witness gives evidence using a device to overcome any disability, disorder or impairment that may affect the ability of the witness to hear or understand the questions and communicate answers.

(b) In giving directions under this section, the court may provide for more than one measure in any particular case.

As previously noted, the decision had been taken by the Group to cover a spectrum of witnesses who, for one reason or another, may meet the definition of "vulnerable witness" in a particular case. This is intended to cover a range of persons, from those who may be traumatised by having to come face - to - face with the defendant to those who may have difficulties with communication by virtue of physical or mental impairment. As a result, it was considered necessary to include a broad range of measures that the court could draw from in giving directions in any particular case. The list was crafted on the basis of this principle, drawing from legislative examples in the UK and New Zealand. The first three of those measures were identified to be of particular importance in cases where face-to-face confrontation with the accused will be very difficult. Thus, it is one of those three measures that the judge will have to apply in the case of a child witness. Other provisions, such as the use of interpreters or devices, could be used in the case of a witness with an impairment affecting the ability to communicate. In addition, the Group recommended that there be a specific provision to reflect that the judge could choose to apply a combination of measures in any particular case.

The majority of the Group was of the view that it would be sufficient to require only the judge, jury, legal counsel and interpreters to be able to see and hear the witness giving evidence from outside the court via technology, without making special provision for the accused being able to see and hear. Others in the Group were concerned that the accused may have a right to personally observe the witness as a part of the right of confrontation. They noted that this will not always be possible where a screen device is used under subsection (a) (depending on the types of screens available), that is because of necessity. In the case of video or other live link, the technology is such in many places that provision can be made for the witness to see and hear only those questioning him or her while all others in the courtroom can see the witness. In light of this difference, some members of the Group felt that the provision should reflect that the accused must also be able to see and hear the witness personally.

Careful consideration should be given to the inclusion of a provision which allows for the admission of video taped cross-examination of the witness. If it can be argued that this requirement hampers the ability of the defence to cross-examine effectively, for example, because it will require cross-examination at an early stage of the proceedings, the legislation may be subject to challenge. Jurisdictions may wish to consider special conditions for the use of this measure such as a higher threshold before it will be ordered or a requirement that the defence must agree with the timing of the cross-examination.

The Group noted that in each jurisdiction, careful consideration would have to be given to what, if any, consequential amendments would be needed to existing legislation in order for these provisions to be effectively implemented. For example, if there is a requirement at law or by statute for trial evidence to be given in the courtroom and not anywhere else, an exception will have to be created for cases where such special measures are ordered, in order that the evidence will be admissible. A good example of how this issue has been dealt with can be seen in the Evidence (Special Provisions) Act No 32 of 1999, Sri Lanka.

The Group noted that, whether by practice or by legislation, the evidence of vulnerable witnesses, particularly children and victims of serious sexual offences, should always be video recorded when given at the first proceeding (preliminary or trial), even in instances where it is not introduced by way of video tape at the proceeding. This is to ensure that if a re-trial becomes necessary for any reason, an application can be made to introduce the tape, as opposed to requiring the witness to testify again. A provision to allow for the introduction of such evidence in the case of a re-trial or subsequent proceeding, either on a discretionary or mandatory basis, should also be included in the law, unless it is already permitted under general rules.

The Group recognised that provisions of this nature, which place restrictions on the manner in which cross-examination will be conducted, could be subject to constitutional challenge. As noted above, some members of the Group were particularly concerned about the effect of such measures on the right of the accused to "confront" his or her accusers. At the same time, it was noted that such challenges have not been successful to date in those jurisdictions where they have been advanced. In addition, the Group was of the view that the fundamental concern with any such provision had to be whether it infringes on the right to a fair trial. In so far as the measures are clearly designed to permit cross-examination and the testing of the evidence, the Group was of the view that arguments that the resulting trial is unfair were unlikely to succeed.

iv. Anonymous witnesses

The Group discussed the possibility of provisions allowing for witness testimony on an anonymous basis. It was noted that in cases of terrorist groups or organised crime, such a provision could be of critical importance, to obtain any witness testimony. On the other hand, the Group was concerned about the impact of such provisions on the rights of the accused and particularly his or her ability to cross-examine fully without knowledge of the identity of the witness. The Group recommended consideration of such provisions but only with appropriate safeguards to protect the rights of the accused, such as the use of an independent counsel for cross-examination of such persons.

v. Questioning of complainant by unrepresented accused

(a) *An accused in a sexual offence or domestic violence case is not entitled to personally cross-examine the complainant or any child witness.*

(b) *An unrepresented accused, who is precluded from personally questioning a witness, may have his or her questions put to the witness by the judge or a person appointed by the judge for that purpose.*

(c) *In respect of each question, the judge may:*
- *(i) put the question or allow the question to be put to the witness;*
- *(ii) put the question or require the question to be put to the witness in a form rephrased by the judge; or*
- *(iii) refuse to put or refuse to allow the question to be put to the witness.*

The Group was of the view that in certain types of cases i.e. sexual offences, child abuse, domestic violence, personal cross-examination by the accused should not be permitted. In some jurisdictions with such a prohibition, there is a requirement for the court to appoint counsel to conduct the cross-examination for the accused. However, the Group recognised that small jurisdictions might not have the resources or capacity to provide counsel in every case of this nature. Thus, the alternative set out in the New Zealand Law Reform Commission Evidence Code was recommended, providing flexibility for either the judge or another person appointed by him or her (which could include counsel) to question the witness.

vi. Complainants in Sexual Offence Cases

The Group considered what legislative restrictions should apply to evidence adduced by way of cross-examination or otherwise in relation to the sexual experience of complainants in sexual assault cases. Three areas of concern were identified: evidence of sexual reputation, prior sexual history generally and prior sexual history with the accused.

The Group determined that any model law in this area would have to strike an appropriate balance between protecting complainants from abuse and further victimisation and preserving the fair trial rights of the accused.

The Group recommended the following content for a model law restricting the evidence to be adduced with respect to complainants in sexual offence cases.

vii. Sexual reputation

In the case of a sexual offence, no evidence can be given and no question can be put to a witness relating directly or indirectly to the reputation of the complainant in sexual matters.

The Group considered that evidence of general sexual reputation should not be permitted. In the opinion of the Group, such evidence could never be relevant to the issues in the case and precluding such evidence would not in any way prejudice the fair trial rights of the accused. At the same time such evidence is highly offensive to the witness and allows for unacceptable inferences to be drawn.

viii. Evidence of prior sexual history with persons other than the accused

In the case of a sexual offence, no evidence can be given and no question can be put to a witness relating directly or indirectly to the sexual experience of the complainant with any person other then the defendant.

The Group held the same view with respect to evidence of sexual experience with persons other than the accused. Despite reflection and discussion, the Group could not think of an instance where such evidence would be relevant to the defence of the accused. Thus, on the basis of the same reasoning as outlined in relation to reputation evidence, the Group recommended that the model law prohibit such evidence.

ix. Sexual experience with the accused

(a) *In the case of a sexual offence, no evidence can be given and no question can be put to a witness relating directly or indirectly to the sexual experience of the complainant with the accused for the purpose of supporting an inference that the complainant:*

(i) is more likely to have consented to the sexual activity that forms the subject matter of the charge or;
(ii) is less worthy of belief.

(b) *For any other purpose, in the case of a sexual offence, no evidence can be given and no question can be put to a witness relating directly or indirectly to the sexual experience of the complainant with the accused, other than in relation to the sexual activity that forms the subject matter of the charge, unless:*

(i) an application for leave is made to the judge, in the absence of the jury; and
(ii) the judge is satisfied that a refusal to allow the evidence to be given or the question to be put would prejudice the fair trial of the accused person.

In the case of evidence of sexual experience with the accused, the Group acknowledged that in some limited circumstances such evidence could be relevant and even critical to the defence and an absolute prohibition could prejudice fair trial rights. At the same time, the Group was of the view that the right to adduce such evidence should not be unlimited but rather should be allowed only where appropriate, as determined by the trial judge. The Group concluded that the evidence should never be allowed to draw the inference of propensity nor for the purposes of general credibility. Where the evidence is to be adduced for other reasons, it should be only with the leave of the court. In addition, because of problems with entrenched views and bias, even within the judiciary, the Group was of the view that there should be a very high threshold for admissibility.

x. Other protective measures in sexual offence cases

(a) *In the case of a sexual offence, the judge shall order a ban on the publication or broadcast of the identity of the complainant or information that could disclose the identity of the complainant, unless the complainant consents to publication or broadcast.*

(b) *The judge may order a ban on the publication or broadcast of the identity of other witnesses or information that could disclose the identity of those witnesses, or order a general ban on publication or broadcast of testimony, where satisfied that it would be in the interests of justice to do so.*

The Group also noted additional measures that should apply in the case of sexual offences. In particular they recommended a mandatory ban on the publication of the identity of the complainant, unless the complainant waives the requirement. In addition, the Group recommended a general discretion for a judge to order a ban on the publication of the identity of other witnesses or a ban on publication of testimony, in cases where it would be in the interests of justice to do so.